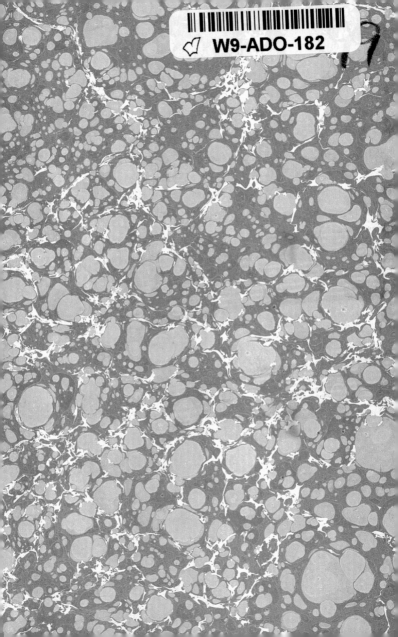

GREAT AMERICAN POETS

GREAT AMERICAN POETS

Edgar Allan Poe

Edited and with an introduction
by Geoffrey Moore

Clarkson N. Potter, Inc./Publishers NEW YORK
DISTRIBUTED BY CROWN PUBLISHERS, INC.

Published in the United States by Clarkson N. Potter, Inc.,
201 East 50th Street, New York, New York 10022
and distributed by Crown Publishers, Inc.
Published in Great Britain by Aurum Press Ltd.,
10 Museum Street, London WC1A 1JS

CLARKSON N. POTTER, POTTER, THE GREAT POETS,
and colophon are trademarks of Clarkson N. Potter, Inc.

Picture research by Juliet Brightmore

Manufactured in China by Imago

Library of Congress Cataloging-in-Publication Data

Poe, Edgar Allan, 1809–1849.
Edgar Allan Poe.

(Great American poets)
I. Moore, Geoffrey. II. Title.
PS2603.M66   1988   811'.3   88–17967
ISBN 0–517–57010–6

10   9   8   7   6   5   4

CONTENTS

INTRODUCTION

Edgar Allan Poe was born in Boston on 19 January 1809, the son of Elizabeth Arnold Poe, an itinerant English actress. Poe's father disappeared soon after he was born, and in 1811 his mother died while on tour in Virginia. The little boy was taken care of by John Allan of Richmond, a tobacco exporter of Scottish extraction.

Between the ages of six and eleven Poe went to school in England, but apart from this he received the normal education of a Virginia gentleman of the time. It was while at the local academy in Richmond that he wrote – if we are to believe him – what has become probably his best-known poem, 'To Helen' (p. 14). At the age of seventeen he enrolled in the University of Virginia but was removed by his adoptive parents a year later because of 'dissolute habits'. The same year he ran away and enlisted in the cavalry under the pseudonym 'Edgar A. Perry'. He rose to the rank of sergeant-major and proceeded to West Point, but after two years in the army he was dishonourably discharged. By this time he had already published two books of verse: *Tamerlane* (1827) and *Al Aaraaf* (1829). From 1831 to 1835 Poe lived in Baltimore with his aunt, Mrs Clemm, whose daughter, Virginia, he married in 1836 when she was thirteen years old.

Following the publication of his third book of verse, *Poems* (1831), Poe broke into the short story market. In the mid-thirties he became editor of the *Southern Literary Messenger,* but friction with his colleagues, due partly to his ideas and partly to his way of life, led to his removal to New York, where he published the memorable

Narrative of Arthur Gordon Pym. He wrote most of his best work before the age of thirty. *The Raven and other Poems and Tales* appeared in 1845.

Two years later, while Poe was working on the mysterious and impressive 'Eureka', his wife died of tuberculosis. In 1849 he returned to Richmond to ask Sarah Royster, a childhood sweetheart, to marry him. Later that year, in a manner entirely consistent with his troubled and irregular life, he was found unconscious in a gutter in Baltimore, drunk or drugged. He died on 7 October 1849.

Poe was the father of the detective story and the macabre 'thriller'. As a poet he was also of great importance, particularly for the late nineteenth-century French writers, to whom he was that great and symbolic figure 'Edgarpo'. For Americans too, constrained as they were by the 'residual pieties' of Puritanism, Poe's poetry showed – as Archibald McLeish said a hundred years later – that 'a poem must not mean but be.'

During his lifetime, however, Poe's peers in America were sceptical of his talent. 'There comes Poe,' said James Russell Lowell in *A Fable for Critics*,

'. . . with his raven, like Barnaby Rudge,
Three fifths of him genius and two fifths sheer fudge,
Who talks like a book of iambs and pentameters,
In a way to make people of common sense damn
    meters,
Who has written some things quite the best of their
    kind,
But the heart somehow seems all squeezed out by the
    mind.'

Fair? Not according to later critics. A fellow Southerner and poet, Allen Tate, showed in 'Our Cousin, Mr Poe' why Poe, so long considered 'meretricious' (T. S. Eliot's term) by Anglo-Saxon commentators, is coming into his own again. 'Eureka', in a sense a long prose poem, and once derided as the work of a madman, is now seen as a remarkable imaginative leap into the area where physics and philosophy meet. That *tour de force* 'The Raven' (p. 36) also achieves an unsuspected power and stature when read in conjunction with 'The Philosophy of Composition', a closely argued commentary showing how the poem was brought into being by a logical formula.

Even the poems which seem at first sight to be purely sentimental reveal themselves on reflection to have a haunting, memorable quality. The 'hard of heart' – to use I. A. Richard's term for those readers who do not fall into the category of 'sentimentalists' – must in the end be wooed by the unafraid nakedness of the feeling. Poe was far from being merely a 'jingle man', as Emerson called him. He was one of the great figures of American literature: timeless and transcendental.

Let W. H. Auden have the last word, for he of all people – highly sceptical as he was – might have been thought the last to be won over. 'No one in his time,' he says of Poe, 'put so much energy and insight into making his contemporary poets take their craft seriously, know what they were doing prosodically, and avoid the faults of slovenly diction and inappropriate imagery that can be avoided by vigilance and hard work.'

GEOFFREY MOORE

A Dream within a Dream

Take this kiss upon the brow!
And, in parting from you now,
Thus much let me avow –
You are not wrong, who deem
That my days have been a dream;
Yet if Hope has flown away
In a night, or in a day,
In a vision, or in none,
Is it therefore the less *gone*?
All that we see or seem
Is but a dream within a dream.

I stand amid the roar
Of a surf-tormented shore,
And I hold within my hand
Grains of the golden sand –
How few! yet how they creep
Through my fingers to the deep,
While I weep – while I weep!
O God! can I not grasp
Them with a tighter clasp?
O God! can I not save
One from the pitiless wave?
Is *all* that we see or seem
But a dream within a dream?

To Helen

Helen, thy beauty is to me
　　Like those Nicéan barks of yore,
That gently, o'er a perfumed sea,
　　The weary, way-worn wanderer bore
　　To his own native shore.

On desperate seas long wont to roam,
　　Thy hyacinth hair, thy classic face,
Thy Naiad airs have brought me home
　　To the glory that was Greece,
And the grandeur that was Rome.

Lo! in yon brilliant window-niche
　　How statue-like I see thee stand,
　　The agate lamp within thy hand!
Ah, Psyche, from the regions which
　　Are Holy Land!

Sonnet – To Science

Science! true daughter of Old Time thou art!
    Who alterest all things with thy peering eyes.
Why preyest thou thus upon the poet's heart,
    Vulture, whose wings are dull realities?
How should he love thee? or how deem thee wise,
    Who wouldst not leave him in his wandering
To seek for treasure in the jewelled skies,
    Albeit he soared with an undaunted wing?
Hast thou not dragged Diana from her car?
    And driven the Hamadryad from the wood
To seek a shelter in some happier star?
    Hast thou not torn the Naiad from her flood,
The Elfin from the green grass, and from me
The summer dream beneath the tamarind tree?

Romance

Romance, who loves to nod and sing,
With drowsy head and folded wing,
Among the green leaves as they shake
Far down within some shadowy lake,
To me a painted paroquet
Hath been – a most familiar bird –
Taught me my alphabet to say,
To lisp my very earliest word,
While in the wild wood I did lie,
A child – with a most knowing eye.

Of late, eternal Condor years
So shake the very Heaven on high
With tumult as they thunder by,
I have no time for idle cares
Through gazing on the unquiet sky.
And when an hour with calmer wings
Its down upon my spirit flings –
That little time with lyre and rhyme
To while away – forbidden things!
My heart would feel to be a crime
Unless it trembled with the strings.

Israfel

And the angel Israfel, whose
heart-strings are a lute, and
who has the sweetest voice
of all God's creatures – KORAN

In Heaven a spirit doth dwell
   'Whose heart-strings are a lute';
None sing so wildly well
As the angel Israfel,
And the giddy stars (so legends tell),
Ceasing their hymns, attend the spell
   Of his voice, all mute.

Tottering above
   In her highest noon,
   The enamoured moon
Blushes with love,
   While, to listen, the red levin
   (With the rapid Pleiads, even,
   Which were seven,)
   Pauses in Heaven.

And they say (the starry choir
 And the other listening things)
That Israfeli's fire
 Is owing to that lyre
 By which he sits and sings –
The trembling living wire
 Of those unusual strings.

But the skies that angel trod,
 Where deep thoughts are a duty –
Where Love's a grown-up God –
 Where the Houri glances are
Imbued with all the beauty
 Which we worship in a star.

Therefore, thou art not wrong,
 Israfeli, who despisest
An unimpassioned song;
To thee the laurels belong,
 Best bard, because the wisest!
Merrily live, and long!

The ecstasies above
    With thy burning measures suit –
Thy grief, thy joy, thy hate, thy love,
    With the fervour of thy lute –
    Well may the stars be mute!

Yes, Heaven is thine; but this
    Is a world of sweets and sours;
    Our flowers are merely – flowers,
And the shadow of thy perfect bliss
    Is the sunshine of ours.

If I could dwell
Where Israfel
    Hath dwelt, and he where I,
He might not sing so wildly well
    A mortal melody,
While a bolder note than this might swell
    From my lyre within the sky.

The City in the Sea

Lo! Death has reared himself a throne
In a strange city lying alone
Far down within the dim West,
Where the good and the bad and the worst and
    the best
Have gone to their eternal rest.
There shrines and palaces and towers
(Time-eaten towers that tremble not!)
Resemble nothing that is ours.
Around, by lifting winds forgot,
Resignedly beneath the sky
The melancholy waters lie.

No rays from the holy heaven come down
On the long night-time of that town;
But light from out the lurid sea
Streams up the turrets silently –
Gleams up the pinnacles far and free –
Up domes – up spires – up kingly halls –
Up fanes – up Babylon-like walls –
Up shadowy long-forgotten bowers
Of sculptured ivy and stone flowers –
Up many and many a marvellous shrine
Whose wreathéd friezes intertwine
The viol, the violet, and the vine.

Resignedly beneath the sky
The melancholy waters lie.

So blend the turrets and shadows there
That all seem pendulous in air,
While from a proud tower in the town
Death looks gigantically down.

There open fanes and gaping graves
Yawn level with the luminous waves;
But not the riches there that lie
In each idol's diamond eye –
Not the gaily-jewelled dead
Tempt the waters from their bed;
For no ripples curl, alas!
Along that wilderness of glass –
No swellings tell that winds may be
Upon some far-off happier sea –
No heavings hint that winds have been
On seas less hideously serene.

But lo, a stir is in the air!
The wave – there is a movement there!
As if the towers had thrust aside,
In slightly sinking, the dull tide –
As if their tops had feebly given
A void within the filmy Heaven.
The waves have now a redder glow –
The hours are breathing faint and low –
And when, amid no earthly moans,
Down, down that town shall settle hence,
Hell, rising from a thousand thrones,
Shall do it reverence.

The Valley of Unrest

*O*nce it smiled a silent dell
Where the people did not dwell;
They had gone unto the wars,
Trusting to the mild-eyed stars,
Nightly, from their azure towers,
To keep watch above the flowers,
In the midst of which all day
The red sun-light lazily lay.
Now each visitor shall confess
The sad valley's restlessness.
Nothing there is motionless –
Nothing save the airs that brood
Over the magic solitude.
Ah, by no wind are stirred those trees
That palpitate like the chill seas
Around the misty Hebrides!
Ah, by no wind those clouds are driven
That rustle through the unquiet Heaven
Uneasily, from morn till even,
Over the violets there that lie
In myriad types of the human eye –
Over the lilies there that wave
And weep above a nameless grave!
They wave: – from out their fragrant tops
Eternal dews come down in drops.
They weep: – from off their delicate stems
Perennial tears descend in gems.

Lenore

Ah, broken is the golden bowl! – the spirit flown
forever!
Let the bell toll! – a saintly soul floats on the
Stygian river: –
And, Guy de Vere, hast *thou* no tear? – weep now
or never more!
See! on yon drear and rigid bier low lies thy love,
Lenore!
Come, let the burial rite be read – the funeral song
be sung! –
An anthem for the queenliest dead that ever died
so young –
A dirge for her the doubly dead in that she died so
young.

'Wretches! ye loved her for her wealth, and ye
hated her for her pride;
And, when she fell in feeble health, ye blessed her –
that she died: –
How *shall* the ritual, then, be read – the requiem
how be sung
By you – by yours, the evil eye, – by yours, the
slanderous tongue
That did to death the innocence that died, and
died so young?'

Peccavimus; yet rave not thus! but let a Sabbath
song

Go up to God so solemnly the dead may feel no
    wrong!
The sweet Lenore hath gone before, with Hope
    that flew beside,
Leaving thee wild for the dear child that should
    have been thy bride –
For her, the fair and debonair, that now so lowly
    lies,
The life upon her yellow hair, but not within her
    eyes –
The life still there upon her hair, the death upon
    her eyes.

'Avaunt! – avaunt! to friends from fiends the
    indignant ghost is riven –
From Hell unto a high estate within the utmost
    Heaven –
From moan and groan to a golden throne beside the
    King of Heaven:–
Let *no* bell toll, then, lest her soul, amid its
    hallowed mirth,
Should catch the note as it doth float up from the
    damnéd Earth!
And I – tonight my heart is light: – no dirge will I
    upraise,
But waft the angel on her flight with a Paean of old
    days!'

To One in Paradise

Thou wast that all to me, love,
   For which my soul did pine –
A green isle in the sea, love,
   A fountain and a shrine,
All wreathed with fairy fruits and flowers,
   And all the flowers were mine.

Ah, dream too bright to last!
   Ah, starry Hope! that didst arise
But to be overcast!
   A voice from out the Future cries,
'On! on!' – but o'er the Past
   (Dim gulf!) my spirit hovering lies
Mute, motionless, aghast!

For, alas! alas! with me
   The light of Life is o'er!
No more – no more – no more –
   (Such language holds the solemn sea
To the sands upon the shore)
   Shall bloom the thunder-blasted tree,
Or the stricken eagle soar!

And all my days are trances,
   And all my nightly dreams
Are where thy grey eye glances,
   And where thy footstep gleams –
In what ethereal dances,
   By what eternal streams.

The Haunted Palace

In the greenest of our valleys,
 By good angels tenanted,
Once a fair and stately palace –
 Radiant palace – reared its head.
In the monarch Thought's dominion –
 It stood there!
Never seraph spread a pinion
 Over fabric half so fair!

Banners yellow, glorious, golden,
 On its roof did float and flow,
(This – all this – was in the olden
 Time long ago,)
And every gentle air that dallied,
 In that sweet day,
Along the ramparts plumed and pallid,
 A winged odor went away.

Wanderers in that happy valley,
 Through two luminous windows, saw
Spirits moving musically
 To a lute's well-tunéd law,
Round about a throne where, sitting,
 Porphyrogene!
In state his glory well befitting,
 The ruler of the realm was seen.

And all with pearl and ruby glowing
    Was the fair palace door,
Through which came flowing, flowing, flowing,
    And sparkling evermore,
A troop of Echoes, whose sweet duty
    Was but to sing,
In voices of surpassing beauty,
    The wit and wisdom of their king.

But evil things, in robes of sorrow,
    Assailed the monarch's high estate.
(Ah, let us mourn! – for never morrow
    Shall dawn upon him, desolate!)
And round about his home the glory
    That blushed and bloomed,
Is but a dim-remembered story
    Of the old time entombed.

And travellers, now, within that valley,
    Through the red-litten windows see
Vast forms that move fantastically
    To a discordant melody,
While, like a ghastly rapid river,
    Through the pale door
A hideous throng rush out forever,
    And laugh – but smile no more.

Sonnet – Silence

There are some qualities – some incorporate
     things,
  That have a double life, which thus is made
A type of that twin entity which springs
  From matter and light, evinced in solid and
     shade.
There is a two-fold *Silence* – sea and shore –
  Body and soul. One dwells in lonely places,
  Newly with grass o'ergrown; some solemn graces,
Some human memories and tearful lore,
Render him terrorless: his name's 'No More'.
He is the corporate Silence: dread him not!
  No power hath he of evil in himself;
But should some urgent fate (untimely lot!)
  Bring thee to meet his shadow (nameless elf,
That haunteth the lone regions where hath trod
No foot of man), commend thyself to God!

Dream-land

By a route obscure and lonely,
Haunted by ill angels only,
Where an Eidolon, named NIGHT,
On a black throne reigns upright,
I have reached these lands but newly
From an ultimate dim Thule –
From a wild weird clime that lieth, sublime,
   Out of SPACE – out of TIME.

Bottomless vales and boundless floods,
And chasms, and caves, and Titan woods,
With forms that no man can discover
For the tears that drip all over;
Mountains toppling evermore
Into seas without a shore;
Seas that restlessly aspire,
Surging, unto skies of fire;
Lakes that endlessly outspread
Their lone waters, lone and dead, –
Their still waters, still and chilly
With the snows of the lolling lily.

By the lakes that thus outspread
Their lone waters, lone and dead, –
Their sad waters, sad and chilly
With the snows of the lolling lily, –
By the mountains – near the river
Murmuring lowly, murmuring ever, –
By the grey woods, – by the swamp

Where the toad and the newt encamp, –
By the dismal tarns and pools
   Where dwell the Ghouls, –
By each spot the most unholy –
In each nook most melancholy, –
There the traveller meets, aghast,
Sheeted Memories of the Past –
Shrouded forms that start and sigh
As they pass the wanderer by –
White-robed forms of friends long given,
In agony, to the Earth – and Heaven.

For the heart whose woes are legion
'T is a peaceful, soothing region –
For the spirit that walks in shadow
'T is – oh, 't is an Eldorado!
But the traveller, travelling through it,
May not – dare not openly view it;
Never its mysteries are exposed
To the weak human eye unclosed;
So wills its King, who hath forbid
The uplifting of the fringéd lid;
And thus the sad Soul that here passes
Beholds it but through darkened glasses.

By a route obscure and lonely,
Haunted by ill angels only,
Where an Eidolon, named NIGHT,
On a black throne reigns upright,
I have wandered home but newly
From this ultimate dim Thule.

The Raven

Once upon a midnight dreary, while I pondered,
    weak and weary,
Over many a quaint and curious volume of
    forgotten lore –
While I nodded, nearly napping, suddenly there
    came a tapping,
As of some one gently rapping, rapping at my
    chamber door.
''T is some visitor,' I muttered, 'tapping at my
    chamber door –
               Only this and nothing more.'

Ah, distinctly I remember it was in the bleak
    December;
And each separate dying ember wrought its ghost
    upon the floor.
Eagerly I wished the morrow; – vainly I had sought
    to borrow
From my books surcease of sorrow – sorrow for the
    lost Lenore –
For the rare and radiant maiden whom the angels
    name Lenore –
               Nameless *here* for evermore.

And the silken, sad, uncertain rustling of each
    purple curtain
Thrilled me – filled me with fantastic terrors never
    felt before;

So that now, to still the beating of my heart, I
    stood repeating,
''T is some visitor entreating entrance at my
    chamber door –
Some late visitor entreating entrance at my
    chamber door; –
              This it is and nothing more.'

Presently my soul grew stronger; hesitating then no
    longer,
'Sir,' said I, 'or Madam, truly your forgiveness I
    implore;
But the fact is I was napping, and so gently you
    came rapping,
And so faintly you came tapping, tapping at my
    chamber door,
That I scarce was sure I heard you' – here I opened
    wide the door; –
              Darkness there and nothing more.

Deep into that darkness peering, long I stood there
    wondering, fearing,
Doubting, dreaming dreams no mortal ever dared
    to dream before;
But the silence was unbroken, and the stillness
    gave no token,
And the only word there spoken was the whispered
    word, 'Lenore?'
This I whispered, and an echo murmured back the
    word, 'Lenore!'
              Merely this and nothing more.

Back into the chamber turning, all my soul within
me burning,
Soon again I heard a tapping somewhat louder than
before.
'Surely,' said I, 'Surely that is something at my
window lattice;
Let me see, then, what thereat is, and this mystery
explore –
Let my heart be still a moment and this mystery
explore; –
　　　　　'T is the wind and nothing more!'

Open here I flung the shutter, when, with many a
flirt and flutter,
In there stepped a stately Raven of the saintly days
of yore;
Not the least obeisance made he; not a minute
stopped or stayed he;
But, with mien of lord or lady, perched above my
chamber door –
Perched upon a bust of Pallas just above my
chamber door –
　　　　　Perched, and sat, and nothing more.

Then this ebony bird beguiling my sad fancy into
smiling,
By the grave and stern decorum of the countenance
it wore,
'Though thy crest be shorn and shaven, thou,' I
said, 'art sure no craven,

Ghastly grim and ancient Raven wandering from
    the Nightly shore –
Tell me what thy lordly name is on the Night's
    Plutonian shore!'
                  Quoth the Raven, 'Nevermore.'

Much I marvelled this ungainly fowl to hear
    discourse so plainly,
Though its answer little meaning – little relevancy
    bore;
For we cannot help agreeing that no living human
    being
Ever yet was blessed with seeing bird above his
    chamber door –
Bird or beast upon the sculptured bust above his
    chamber door,
                  With such name as 'Nevermore'.

But the Raven, sitting lonely on the placid bust,
    spoke only
That one word, as if his soul in that one word he
    did outpour.
Nothing farther then he uttered – not a feather
    then he fluttered –
Till I scarcely more than muttered, 'Other friends
    have flown before –
On the morrow *he* will leave me, as my Hopes have
    flown before.'
                  Then the bird said, 'Nevermore.'

Startled at the stillness broken by reply so aptly
　　spoken,
'Doubtless,' said I, 'what it utters is its only stock
　　and store
Caught from some unhappy master whom
　　unmerciful Disaster
Followed fast and followed faster till his songs one
　　burden bore –
Till the dirges of his Hope that melancholy burden
　　bore
　　　　　　　　Of '"Never – nevermore."'

But the Raven still beguiling my sad fancy into
　　smiling,
Straight I wheeled a cushioned seat in front of bird
　　and bust and door;
Then, upon the velvet sinking, I betook myself to
　　linking
Fancy unto fancy, thinking what this ominous bird
　　of yore –
What this grim, ungainly, ghastly, gaunt, and
　　ominous bird of yore
　　　　　　　　Meant in croaking 'Nevermore.'

This I sat engaged in guessing, but no syllable
　　expressing
To the fowl whose fiery eyes now burned into my
　　bosom's core;
This and more I sat divining, with my head at ease
　　reclining
On the cushion's velvet lining that the lamp-light
　　gloated o'er,

But whose velvet-violet lining with the lamp-light
     gloating o'er,

    She shall press, ah, nevermore!

Then, methought, the air grew denser, perfumed
     from an unseen censer
Swung by seraphim whose foot-falls tinkled on the
     tufted floor.
'Wretch,' I cried, 'thy God hath lent thee – by
     these angels he hath sent thee
Respite – respite and nepenthe from thy memories
     of Lenore;
Quaff, oh, quaff this kind nepenthe and forget this
     lost Lenore!'

    Quoth the Raven, 'Nevermore.'

'Prophet!' said I, 'thing of evil – prophet still, if
     bird or devil! –
Whether Tempter sent, or whether tempest tossed
     thee here ashore,
Desolate yet all undaunted, on this desert land
     enchanted –
On this home by Horror haunted – tell me truly, I
     implore –
Is there – *is* there balm in Gilead? – tell me – tell
     me, I implore!'

    Quoth the Raven, 'Nevermore.'

'Prophet!' said I, 'thing of evil – prophet still, if
     bird or devil!
By that Heaven that bends above us – by that God
     we both adore –

Tell this soul with sorrow laden if, within the
    distant Aidenn,
It shall clasp a sainted maiden whom the angels
    name Lenore –
Clasp a rare and radiant maiden whom the angels
    name Lenore.'
                  Quoth the Raven, 'Nevermore.'

'Be that word our sign of parting, bird or fiend!' I
    shrieked, upstarting –
'Get thee back into the tempest and the Night's
    Plutonian shore!
Leave no black plume as a token of that lie thy soul
    hath spoken!
Leave my loneliness unbroken! – quit the bust
    above my door!
Take thy beak from out my heart, and take thy
    form from off my door!'
                  Quoth the Raven, 'Nevermore.'

And the Raven, never flitting, still is sitting, *still* is
    sitting
On the pallid bust of Pallas just above my chamber
    door;
And his eyes have all the seeming of a demon's that
    is dreaming,
And the lamp-light o'er him streaming throws his
    shadow on the floor;
And my soul from out that shadow that lies floating
    on the floor
                Shall be lifted – nevermore!

The Bells

I

Hear the sledges with the bells –
Silver bells!
What a world of merriment their melody foretells!
How they tinkle, tinkle, tinkle,
In the icy air of night!
While the stars that oversprinkle
All the heavens, seem to twinkle
With a crystalline delight;
Keeping time, time, time,
In a sort of Runic rhyme,
To the tintinnabulation that so musically wells
From the bells, bells, bells, bells,
Bells, bells, bells –
From the jingling and the tinkling of the bells.

II

Hear the mellow wedding bells –
Golden bells!
What a world of happiness their harmony foretells!
Through the balmy air of night
How they ring out their delight! –
From the molten-golden notes,
And all in tune,
What a liquid ditty floats
To the turtle-dove that listens, while she gloats
On the moon!

Oh, from out the sounding cells,
What a gush of euphony voluminously wells!
How it swells!
How it dwells
On the Future! – how it tells
Of the rapture that impels
To the swinging and the ringing
Of the bells, bells, bells,
Of the bells, bells, bells, bells,
Bells, bells, bells, –
To the rhyming and the chiming of the bells!

III

Hear the loud alarum bells –
Brazen bells!
What a tale of terror, now, their turbulency tells!
In the startled ear of night
How they scream out their affright!
Too much horrified to speak,
They can only shriek, shriek,
Out of tune,
In a clamorous appealing to the mercy of the fire,
In a mad expostulation with the deaf and frantic fire,
Leaping higher, higher, higher,
With a desperate desire,
And a resolute endeavor
Now – now to sit, or never,
By the side of the pale-faced moon.

Oh, the bells, bells, bells!
What a tale their terror tells
Of despair!
How they clang, and clash, and roar!
What a horror they outpour
On the bosom of the palpitating air!
Yet the ear it fully knows,
By the twanging
And the clanging,
How the danger ebbs and flows;
Yet the ear distinctly tells,
In the jangling
And the wrangling,
How the danger sinks and swells,
By the sinking or the swelling in the anger of the bells –
Of the bells, –
Of the bells, bells, bells, bells,
Bells, bells, bells –
In the clamor and the clangor of the bells!

IV

Hear the tolling of the bells –
Iron bells!
What a world of solemn thought their monody compels!
In the silence of the night,
How we shiver with affright
At the melancholy menace of their tone!

For every sound that floats
From the rust within their throats
      Is a groan.
And the people – ah, the people –
They that dwell up in the steeple,
      All alone,
  And who tolling, tolling, tolling,
    In that muffled monotone,
  Feel a glory in so rolling
    On the human heart a stone –
They are neither man nor woman –
They are neither brute nor human –
    They are Ghouls: –
And their king it is who tolls: –
And he rolls, rolls, rolls,
      Rolls
  A paean from the bells!
And his merry bosom swells
  With the paean of the bells!
And he dances, and he yells;
Keeping time, time, time,
In a sort of Runic rhyme,
  To the paean of the bells –
    Of the bells: –
Keeping time, time, time,
In a sort of Runic rhyme,
  To the throbbing of the bells –

Of the bells, bells, bells –
　　To the sobbing of the bells;
Keeping time, time, time,
　　As he knells, knells, knells,
In a happy Runic rhyme,
　　To the rolling of the bells –
Of the bells, bells, bells: –
　　To the tolling of the bells –
Of the bells, bells, bells, bells,
　　Bells, bells, bells –
To the moaning and the groaning of the bells.

For Annie

Thank Heaven! the crisis,
    The danger, is past,
And the lingering illness
    Is over at last –
And the fever called 'Living'
    Is conquered at last.

Sadly, I know
    I am shorn of my strength,
And no muscle I move
    As I lie at full length –
But no matter! – I feel
    I am better at length.

And I rest so composedly,
    Now, in my bed,
That any beholder
    Might fancy me dead –
Might start at beholding me,
    Thinking me dead.

The moaning and groaning,
    The sighing and sobbing,
Are quieted now,
    With that horrible throbbing
At heart: – ah, that horrible,
    Horrible throbbing!

The sickness – the nausea –
    The pitiless pain –

Have ceased, with the fever
   That maddened my brain
With the fever called 'Living'
   That burned in my brain.

And oh! of all tortures
   That torture the worst
Has abated – the terrible
   Torture of thirst
For the naphthaline river
   Of Passion accurst: –
I have drank of a water
   That quenches all thirst: –

Of a water that flows,
   With a lullaby sound,
From a spring but a very few
   Feet under ground –
From a cavern not very far
   Down under ground.

And ah! let it never
   Be foolishly said
That my room it is gloomy
   And narrow my bed;
For man never slept
   In a different bed –
And, to *sleep*, you must slumber
   In just such a bed.

My tantalized spirit
   Here blandly reposes,
Forgetting, or never
   Regretting, its roses –
Its old agitations
   Of myrtles and roses:

For now, while so quietly
   Lying, it fancies
A holier odor
   About it, of pansies –
A rosemary odor,
   Commingled with pansies –
With rue and the beautiful
   Puritan pansies.

And so it lies happily,
   Bathing in many
A dream of the truth
   And the beauty of Annie –
Drowned in a bath
   Of the tresses of Annie.

She tenderly kissed me,
   She fondly caressed,
And then I fell gently
   To sleep on her breast –
Deeply to sleep
   From the heaven of her breast.

When the light was extinguished,
   She covered me warm,

And she prayed to the angels
    To keep me from harm –
To the queen of the angels
    To shield me from harm.

And I lie so composedly,
    Now, in my bed,
(Knowing her love),
    That you fancy me dead –
And I rest so contentedly,
    Now, in my bed
(With her love at my breast),
    That you fancy me dead –
That you shudder to look at me,
    Thinking me dead: –

But my heart it is brighter
    Than all of the many
Stars in the sky,
    For it sparkles with Annie –
It glows with the light
    Of the love of my Annie –
With the thought of the light
    Of the eyes of my Annie.

To My Mother

Because I feel that, in the Heavens above,
   The angels, whispering to one another,
Can find, among their burning terms of love,
   None so devotional as that of 'Mother',
Therefore by that dear name I long have called you –
   You who are more than mother unto me,
And fill my heart of hearts, where Death installed you
   In setting my Virginia's spirit free.
My mother – my own mother, who died early,
   Was but the mother of myself; but you
Are mother to the one I loved so dearly,
   And thus are dearer than the mother I knew
By that infinity with which my wife
   Was dearer to my soul than its soul-life.

Annabel Lee

It was many and many a year ago,
    In a kingdom by the sea,
That a maiden there lived whom you may know
    By the name of Annabel Lee;
And this maiden she lived with no other thought
    Than to love and be loved by me.

She was a child and *I* was a child,
    In this kingdom by the sea,
But we loved with a love that was more than love –
    I and my Annabel Lee –
With a love that the wingéd seraphs of Heaven
    Coveted her and me.

And this was the reason that, long ago,
    In this kingdom by the sea,
A wind blew out a cloud by night
    Chilling my Annabel Lee;
So that her highborn kinsmen came
    And bore her away from me,
To shut her up in a sepulchre
    In this kingdom by the sea.

The angels, not half so happy in Heaven,
    Went envying her and me: –
Yes! – that was the reason (as all men know,
    In this kingdom by the sea)
That the wind came out of the cloud, chilling
    And killing my Annabel Lee.

But our love it was stronger by far than the love
  Of those who were older than we –
  Of many far wiser than we –
And neither the angels in Heaven above
  Nor the demons down under the sea,
Can ever dissever my soul from the soul
  Of the beautiful Annabel Lee: –

For the moon never beams, without bringing me dreams
  Of the beautiful Annabel Lee;
And the stars never rise but I see the bright eyes
  Of the beautiful Annabel Lee:
And so, all the night-tide, I lie down by the side
Of my darling, my darling, my life and my bride,
  In the sepulchre there by the sea –
  In her tomb by the side of the sea.

NOTES ON THE PICTURES

Edmund Dulac (1882–1953) was a prolific illustrator and a man of many talents: composer, writer, designer, draughtsman and watercolourist.

The watercolours in this book are taken from *The Bells and Other Poems* by *Edgar Allan Poe*, illustrated by Edmund Dulac, 1912, and are reproduced by permission of Hodder and Stoughton Ltd.

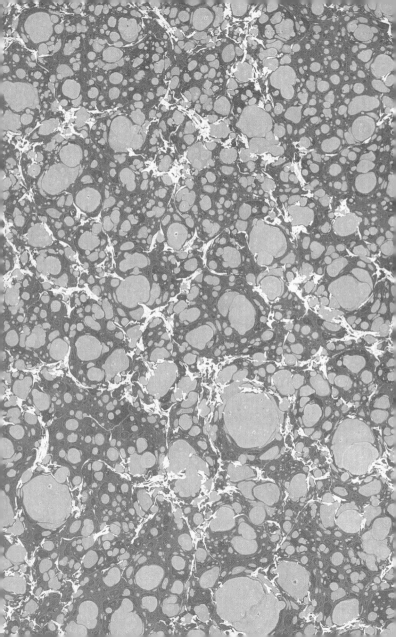